TABLE of CONTENTS

Chapter 1
BIRTH OF A LEGEND 4

Chapter 2
THE CHASE IS ON! 6

Chapter 3
CAN HE DO IT? 18

THE LEGACY OF BABE RUTH 28

GLOSSARY 30

READ MORE 31

INTERNET SITES 31

INDEX 32

WITHDRAWN

BABE RUTH

Birth Of a Legend

George Herman "Babe" Ruth Jr. began his major league baseball career as a pitcher with the Boston Red Sox in 1914. The 19-year-old southpaw quickly became one of the best hurlers in the game. In 1915 he won 18 games. The next year he won 23. In 1917 Ruth notched a career-high 24 victories.

The Red Sox became a great team. They won the World Series in 1915, 1916, and 1918.

But Ruth was also an amazing hitter. In 1919 he hit an astounding 29 home runs, breaking a record that was set in 1884.

But in 1920 Harry Frazee, the owner of the Red Sox, needed money for his other businesses. He sold Ruth's contract to the New York Yankees.

Ruth became a full-time outfielder for the Yanks.

In his first year with the Yankees, Ruth crushed 54 home runs. In 1921 he stunned the baseball world by belting 59 round-trippers.

Every season after that, Ruth tried to top his home run mark.

You gonna break the record this year, Babe?

I sure will, fellas. I promise!

I've got to do it. The kids are counting on me.

But the years passed, and it didn't happen. Would he ever do it?

The Chase Is On!

By 1927 Ruth still hadn't broken his record. But he had become the most famous man in America.

RUTH'S **HOME RUN** CANDY BAR

BABE RUTH *Says* "IT'S THE FINEST COLA DRINK I EVER TASTED"

Babe loved being in the limelight. He appeared in movies and advertisements. Newspapers across the country reported Ruth's every move. Americans couldn't get enough of their favorite slugger.

In March 1927 Ruth signed a contract with Yankee owner Jacob Ruppert. Babe would get $70,000 a year to continue playing for the Yanks.

Babe, you're the highest-paid player in baseball. We're counting on you to help us win some championships!

That's what I'm here for, Mr. Ruppert!

When the 1927 season began, the pressure to break the record of 59 home runs was greater than ever.

Do you think you can do it, Babe?

I may not ever break the 1921 record. I get more bad pitches to hit than any other player.

Despite Ruth's doubts about setting a new record, no one doubted that the 1927 Yankees were a great team.

The hard-hitting Yankee lineup had been nicknamed "Murderers' Row."

Earle Combs

Babe Ruth

Bob Meusel

Lou Gehrig

Tony Lazzeri

Mark Koenig

Joe Dugan

Powerful first baseman Lou Gehrig was a key member of Murderers' Row. Gehrig had joined the Yanks in 1923 and showed lots of promise. In 1925 he belted 20 homers. In 1926 he hit 16.

Gehrig would have one of his best seasons in 1927. So would Ruth.

The Yankees opened the 1927 season against the Philadelphia Athletics at Yankee Stadium.

Ruth didn't wait long to begin his quest for the home run record. On April 15, in the fourth game of the series, Ruth smashed his first home run of the season.

Ruth kept pounding the long ball throughout April and May. On May 31, against the Athletics, he whacked homer number 15 in the first game of a doubleheader.

Ruth then crushed number 16 in the second game. The ball soared completely out of the stadium. Amazingly, it cleared a two-story house across the street.

In front of 30,000 fans at Yankee Stadium on June 11, Ruth walloped home run number 19.

The blast cleared the fence in straightaway center field. It landed just in front of the huge scoreboard.

The ball traveled so far that Cleveland Indians catcher Luke Sewell suspected foul play.

Lemme see that club!

Nobody could hit one like that without having a slug of lead or something in the end of his bat!

Sewell didn't find anything wrong with Ruth's bat.

Two innings later Ruth pounded his 20th homer. His teammate Lou Gehrig had 14 home runs on the season.

Ruth wasn't the only one chasing history in America that spring. In May Charles Lindbergh became the first person to fly an airplane solo across the Atlantic Ocean.

Parades and celebrations were held in his honor everywhere.

I wonder what's holding up the start of the game?

I think they're waiting for Lindbergh to get here.

Lindbergh had been invited to Yankee Stadium to attend a June 16 game against the St. Louis Browns.

But by game time, he had not shown up.

The umpires decided to delay the game until Lindbergh arrived. Meanwhile, in the Yankee dugout …

I feel a homer coming.

My left ear itches. That's a sure sign.

After waiting 30 minutes, the umpires finally ordered to start the game without Lindbergh.

In the first inning, Ruth slammed home run number 22 into the bleachers.

After the game Ruth met with reporters.

That was some shot, Babe.

I had been saving that homer for Lindbergh. I held back as long as I could.

When you get one of those things in your system, it's bound to come out.

Meanwhile, Gehrig chased Ruth for the home run lead.

On June 29, against the Boston Red Sox in Fenway Park, Gehrig slammed a round-tripper to finally catch Ruth. They were tied at 24 homers each. Ruth had never had competition like this before.

The home run race seesawed back and forth throughout July.

But on July 28, at home against the St. Louis Browns, Ruth struck again. He crushed his 34th homer. It put him one ahead of Gehrig.

The excitement about the home run race between Ruth and Gehrig was building. Yankee manager Miller Huggins talked to the press about his two star sluggers.

How would you compare their swings, coach?

The Babe swings with a free motion of his wrists, and the swing comes from right out of his powerful shoulders.

Lou, on the other hand, hits with a rigid wrist ... he's in a position to get more direct power from his drives.

The differences in the sluggers' hitting styles resulted in different kinds of home runs. Ruth often hit towering, soaring arcs. Gehrig usually smacked hard line drives.

On August 16 Ruth proved that no pitcher—or ballpark—could contain him. At Comiskey Park in Chicago, he launched a monster home run completely out of the huge stadium.

At the end of the game, more than 5,000 young fans poured onto the field to congratulate Ruth. It was his 37th homer. Gehrig had 38.

You Chicago fans are all right in my book!

The home run race between the two teammates continued through August. By the end of the month, Ruth led Gehrig, 43-41. With only 28 games remaining in the season, Ruth needed 17 homers to break his record.

Time was running out.

Ruth and Gehrig were tied at 44 home runs as they entered the September 6 doubleheader at Boston's Fenway Park.

In the fifth inning of the first game, Gehrig drilled his 45th round-tripper. In the sixth inning, Ruth hit one. Then Ruth added his 46th homer in the seventh. In the second game, Ruth blasted another homer. He now led Gehrig, 47-45.

The New York Times reported, "… for the moment, at least, the master home-run swatter of the age still is George Herman Ruth."

But Ruth wasn't finished roughing up Red Sox pitching. On September 7 he slammed two more bombs for numbers 48 and 49.

Ruth's five homers in two days knocked Gehrig out of the home run race. Gehrig would hit only two more homers the rest of the year. Now Ruth had the stage all to himself.

Way to go, Babe! Now you've got 21 games to hit 11 homers!

Could he do it?

As the month rolled on, Ruth continued to hit the long ball. By September 22 he had 55 homers when he took the field against the Detroit Tigers at Yankee Stadium.

In the bottom of the ninth inning, the Yanks were down by one run. But with no one out and a man on first base, Ruth took care of business. In one mammoth swing, he crushed home run number 56 deep into the right-field bleachers.

As Ruth went into his home run trot …

Babe! Babe! Gimme your bat!

Get off the field, kid!

Let go of it, Babe! Let go!

Get off my bat, son!

I gotta get off the field before this kid gets hurt!

W-whoa!! L-let go, Babe!

For the last time, kid— let go of my bat!

The New York Times reported, "… the youngster was like the tail of a flying comet holding onto the bat for dear life …"

The afternoon ended with lots of laughs. Ruth now had only six games to hit four homers.

Can He Do It?

Ruth failed to put one in the seats in the next two games against Detroit. But on September 27 he found his stroke against the Philadelphia Athletics. In the bottom of the sixth inning, he smashed a grand slam against pitcher Lefty Grove. It was Ruth's 57th homer of the year.

He had only three games left to hit three homers.

On September 29 Ruth continued to swing a hot bat. At home against the Washington Senators, he launched his 58th home run in the first inning. Then, in the fifth inning, he crushed number 59 to tie his 1921 record.

Ruth had two games left to top that record.

Leading off the bottom of the eighth inning, Yankee shortstop Mark Koenig ripped a shot deep into the outfield.

The next day, the Yankees faced Washington's Tom Zachary. The lefty kept the Yanks' bats at bay. After seven and a half innings, the score was knotted at 2-2.

Koenig sped around the bases and safely pulled into third with a long triple.

Ruth was up next. He carried one of his favorite bats, which he called "Beautiful Bella."

Ruth had already faced Zachary three times in the game. He walked and singled twice.

During the season, Ruth had hit two homers off Zachary.

The pitcher was determined not to give up another one.

Zachary's first pitch was a blazing fastball …

Strike one!

Zachary threw Ruth another fastball …

High … ball one.

Ruth carefully dug in for the next pitch.

Zachary stared in for a sign from the Senators' catcher.

Curveball.

Ruth waited for Zachary's next offering ...

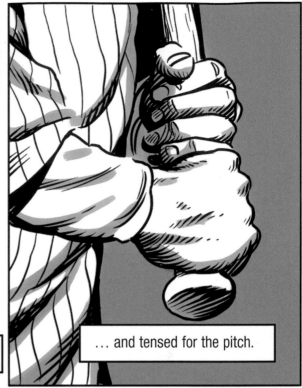

... and tensed for the pitch.

On the 1-1 count, the Senator pitcher hurled the ball low and inside.

Ruth pounced on it ...

CRACKK!

The three men stood frozen, following the flight of Ruth's vicious blast.

Stay fair! Stay fair!

FAIR BALL!!!

Hoo-ha!

The crowd erupted in wild celebration. Yankee Stadium shook from the thunderous pounding of stomping feet.

The New York Times reported, "… the bat connected with a crash that was audible in all parts of the stand … Number 60 was some homer, a fitting wallop to top the Babe's record of 59 in 1921."

The only unhappy person at Yankee Stadium was Tom Zachary.

It was a foul ball! A foul ball!

The ball was fair. Get ready to pitch to the next batter.

"While the crowd cheered and the Yankee players roared their greetings the Babe made his triumphant, almost regal, tour of the paths," said *The New York Times.*

Even Yankee third base coach, Charlie O'Leary, joined in the celebration.

What do you think about that, Charlie?

Woo-hoo!

Many years later one writer said, "George Herman Ruth did more than just smack 60 home runs in 1927. He achieved a Ruthian feat."

And with it Babe Ruth achieved a place in both baseball and American history.

The Legacy of Babe Ruth

George Herman Ruth was born February 6, 1895, in Baltimore, Maryland. He picked up the name "Babe" in 1914 as a young player for the Baltimore Orioles of the International League. Other players began referring to him as the "newest babe" of Jack Dunn, the Orioles owner. The name stuck. Over the years he picked up many other nicknames. They included "The Sultan of Swat," "The Bambino," "The King of Clout," and "The Colossus of Crash."

The 1927 Yankees ended the season with 110 wins, 44 losses, and one tie. Only four teams in baseball history have won more games in a single season. The Yankees crushed the Pittsburgh Pirates in the 1927 World Series, sweeping them four games to none. Ruth led the Yanks' assault, batting .400 with two homers and seven runs batted in.

Before Ruth's homer heroics, baseball was played differently than it is today. Batters were content to hit singles and doubles. Ruth's single-season home run record stood for 34 years. In 1961 New York Yankee Roger Maris hit 61 homers in a 162-game season. When Ruth retired from baseball in 1935, he had hit more home runs than anyone, 714. His record stood until 1974, when Hank Aaron hit his 715th.

RUTH IN THE YANKEE DUGOUT

RUTH 1921

In 1936 Ruth was one of the first five players elected to the Baseball Hall of Fame. To this day he is widely regarded as the greatest player of all time. He died on August 16, 1948, at the age of 53.

GLOSSARY

audible (AW-duh-buhl)—loud enough to be heard

comet (KOM-uht)—a ball of rock and ice that circles the sun

curveball (KURV-bawl)—a pitch that spins away from a straight path as it approaches the batter

double (DUH-buhl)—a hit that allows a player to get to second base

doubleheader (DUH-buhl HED-ur)—two baseball games played one right after the other

erupt (i-RUHPT)—to release or force out suddenly

hurler (HURL-uhr)—a baseball pitcher

limelight (LIME-lite)—the center of attention

line drive (LINE DRIVE)—a batted baseball that is hit in a nearly straight line, usually not far above the ground

mammoth (MAM-uhth)—huge

notch (NOCH)—to mark or record

regal (REE-guhl)—to do with or fit for a king or queen

round-tripper (ROUND-TRIP-uhr)—a home run

shortstop (SHORT-stop)—the defensive position between second and third base in baseball

single (SING-guhl)—a hit that allows a runner to get to first base

slugger (SLUHG-uhr)—a hard-hitting batter in baseball

southpaw (SOUTH-paw)—a left-handed pitcher

triple (TRIP-uhl)—a hit that allows a runner to get to third base

vicious (VISH-uhss)—fierce or dangerous

READ MORE

Christopher, Matt. *Babe Ruth.* Legends in Sports. London: Little, Brown and Company, 2005.

Fischer, David. *Babe Ruth: Legendary Slugger.* Sterling Biographies New York: Sterling Books, 2010.

Kelly, David A. *Babe Ruth and the Baseball Curse.* New York: Random House, 2009.

INTERNET SITES

FactHound offers a safe, fun way to find Internet sites related to this book. All of the sites on FactHound have been researched by our staff.

Here's all you do: Visit *www.facthound.com*

Type in this code: 9781429654739

Check out projects, games and lots more at
www.CAPSTONEKIDS.com

INDEX

Aaron, Hank, 29

Baltimore Orioles, 28
Baseball Hall of Fame, 29
Boston Red Sox, 4, 5, 12, 15

Cleveland Indians, 9
Combs, Earle, 7
Comiskey Park, 14

Detroit Tigers, 16, 18
Dugan, Joe, 7
Dunn, Jack, 28

Fenway Park, 12, 15
Frazee, Harry, 5

Gehrig, Lou, 7, 9, 12, 13, 14, 15
Grove, Lefty, 18

Huggins, Miller, 13

Koenig, Mark, 7, 19

Lazzeri, Tony, 7
Lindbergh, Charles, 10, 11

Maris, Roger, 29
Meusel, Bob, 7
Murderers' Row, 7

New York Times, The, 15, 17, 25, 26

O'Leary, Charlie, 27

Philadelphia Athletics, 8, 18
Pittsburgh Pirates, 28

Ruppert, Jacob, 6
Ruth, George Herman "Babe" Jr.,
   birth of, 28
   death of, 29
   nicknames of, 28
   pitching career of, 4
   public life of, 6

Sewell, Luke, 9
St. Louis Browns, 10, 12

Washington Senators, 18, 22
World Series, 4, 28

Yankee Stadium, 8, 9, 10, 16, 25, 26

Zachary, Tom, 19, 20–23, 26

AMERICAN GRAPHIC

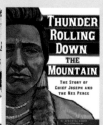